Z is

for Moose

BY KELLY BINGHAM

PICTURES BY PAUL O. ZELINSKY

SCHOLASTIC INC.

ISBN 978-0-545-54421-4

Text copyright © 2012 by Kelly Bingham.
Illustrations copyright © 2012 by Paul O. Zelinsky.
All rights reserved. Published by Scholastic Inc., 557 Broadway, New York, NY 10012, by arrangement with Greenwillow Books, an imprint of HarperCollins Publishers. SCHOLASTIC and associated logos are trademarks and/or registered trademarks of Scholastic Inc.

12 11 10 9 8 7 6 5   14 15 16 17 18/0

Printed in the U.S.A.   40

First Scholastic printing, January 2013

Mixed media were used to prepare the full-color art.
The text type is Times Roman.

For Sam, who asked for a funny book,
and for Benny, because I love you too—K.B.

♥ is for Rachel—P. O. Z.

A is for Apple

B is for Ball

C is for Cat

F is for Fox

G is for Glove

I is for Ice Cream

J is for Jar

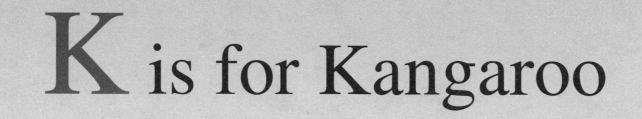

L is for Lollipop

N is for Needle

Tis for Truck

U is for Umbrella

V is for Violin

W is for Whale

X is for Xylophone

Z is for
Zebra's friend, Moose

A B C D E F G H I J K L M N O P Q R S T U V W X Y Z

The End